Pink
Takes a
Bow

by Christianne C. Jones

illustrated by Todd Ouren

Special thanks to our advisers for their expertise:

Linda Frichtel, Design Adjunct Faculty
Minneapolis College of Art & Design

Terry Flaherty, Ph.D., Professor of English
Minnesota State University, Mankato

PICTURE WINDOW BOOKS
Minneapolis, Minnesota

Editor: Jill Kalz
Designer: Hilary Wacholz
Page Production: Melissa Kes
Art Director: Nathan Gassman
The illustrations in this book were created digitally.

Picture Window Books
5115 Excelsior Boulevard
Suite 232
Minneapolis, MN 55416
877-845-8392
www.picturewindowbooks.com

Printed in the United States of America.

All books published by Picture Window Books
are manufactured with paper containing at least
10 percent post-consumer waste.

Library of Congress Cataloging-in-Publication Data
Jones, Christianne C.
Pink takes a bow / by Christianne C. Jones ; illustrated by
Todd Ouren.
p. cm. — (Know your colors)
ISBN-13: 978-1-4048-3763-8 (library binding)
ISBN-10: 1-4048-3763-9 (library binding)
1. Pink—Juvenile literature. 2. Colors—Juvenile literature.
I. Ouren, Todd, ill. II. Title.
QC495.5J6588 2008
535.6—dc22   2007004274

The World is filled with COLORS.

Colors are either primary or secondary. Red, yellow, and blue are primary colors. These are the colors that can't be made by mixing two other colors together. Orange, purple, and green are secondary colors. Secondary colors are made by mixing together two primary colors.

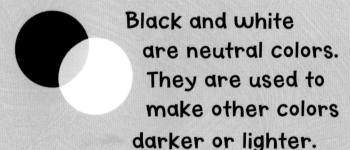

BLUE
PURPLE
GREEN
YELLOW
RED
ORANGE

Black and white are neutral colors. They are used to make other colors darker or lighter.

Red + White   =   Pink

Pink doesn't fit into any of these groups. Pink is a shade, or tint, of red. Mixing red and white makes pink.

Keep your eyes open for colorful fun!

4

The color **PINK** can twirl, jump, and spin.

A dance recital makes everyone grin.

Silky **PINK** ribbons tie hair nice and tight.

Little **PINK** shoes are laced up right.

Frilly **PINK** skirts line up in a row.

Rosy **PINK** cheeks are all aglow.

14

Thick **PINK** curtains open with a flash.

Pretty **PINK** costumes go down with a CRASH!

Clumsy **PINK** birds get tangled and stuck.

Chubby **PINK** pigs have tons of bad luck.

The recital was a mess, but the kids had fun.

Where else does **PINK** play when the show is done?

MAKING PINK

WHAT YOU NEED:
- red paint
- paper plates
- white paint
- paintbrushes

WHAT YOU DO:
1. Place one drop of red paint on a paper plate.
2. Add a few drops of white paint to the red paint.
3. Mix the red and white paint together with a brush. You've made pink!
4. Now, try the activity again. This time, add just one drop of white paint to the drop of red. How is this pink different from the first pink you made?

FUN FACTS

- In some parts of the world, the color pink is only for little girls. It is often thought of as a feminine, delicate color.

- For many people, pink is the color of love. It means romance and charm.

- Walter Diemer invented pink-colored Double Bubble bubble gum in 1928. It was pink because pink was the only color of food coloring he had.

- A pink carnation (a kind of flower) means "I will never forget you."

TO LEARN MORE

AT THE LIBRARY

Brown, Margaret Wise. *My World of Color.* New York: Hyperion Books for Children, 2002.

Dahl, Michael. *Pink: Seeing Pink All Around Us.* Mankato, Minn.: Capstone Press, 2005.

Thomas, Isabel. *Pink Foods.* Chicago: Heinemann, 2005.

ON THE WEB

FactHound offers a safe, fun way to find Web sites related to this book. All of the sites on FactHound have been researched by our staff.

1. Visit www.facthound.com
2. Type in this special code: 1404837639
3. Click on the FETCH IT button.

Your trusty FactHound will fetch the best sites for you!

Look for all of the books in the Know Your Colors series:

Autumn Orange

Batty for Black

Big Red Farm

Brown at the Zoo

Camping in Green

Hello, Yellow!

Pink Takes a Bow

Purple Pride

Splish, Splash, and Blue

Winter White